There's
MORE
THAN ONE
F-WORD

Redefining Success
one F-Word at a time

Beth Townsend & Rhett Townsend

MH

MICHTER HOUSE
PUBLISHING

an imprint of
Rope Swing Publishing

ISBN: 978-1-964026-02-2 (paperback)
ISBN: 978-1-964026-03-9 (ebook)

There's More Than One F-Word

MH

MICHTER HOUSE
PUBLISHING
an imprint of
Rope Swing Publishing

www.ropeswingpublishing.com

Table of Contents

Foreword

Fred Townsend

In a time long ago, and a place faraway. When the Empire Struck Back. And the only heavy breathing on motion picture screens was Darth Vader.

Before streaming.

Before cell phones and texting.

Before the internet.

When Carrie Fisher was still hot, and Harrison Ford was a young action star.

There was a time Millennials never knew and Baby-Boomers can't remember without a dose of Focus Factor. People talked on "land-lines telephones." That is, phones that were plugged into phone lines installed in the walls of homes. It's hard to believe it now, but if people had something to say to one another, someone dialed a number and waited to find out if the other person would answer and therefore be available to converse.

In that era, my brother Steve was already an accomplished sportswriter, en route to a successful career that included authoring multiple books and piling a stack of noteworthy awards. His phone call to me that Sunday afternoon was one that I will never forget. It was only minutes after he'd interviewed an All-American college football player for a magazine article. As an aside, the player went on to a storied NFL career.

While neither my brother nor I graduated *Summa Cum Laude*, we weren't at the bottom of our respective graduating classes either. Frankly, we had excellent vocabularies. Both of our parents, though not well-educated, were prolific readers and we had followed suit. In fact, we had the same 7th grade English teacher as our dad. Maude Bullock, was a drill sergeant when it came to understanding how to diagram a sentence. Which brings me to my point and to the reason for that phone call.

There are eight principal "parts of speech" in the English language: *Noun, Pronoun, Verb, Adjective, Adverb, Preposition, Conjunction,* and *Interjection.* After careful analysis, Steve reckoned that the interviewee had used the F-word as all eight parts of speech. Several times. By any analysis, noteworthy. Steve had to tell somebody! It was so unbelievable that not sharing it would have been tantamount to covering up evidence in the Kennedy assassination.

Now it took an active imagination to figure out how to make an adverb out of the F-word. And, admittedly, the All-American athlete had to combine the f-word to create compound words for his purposes. Let me also note the football star was NOT an *Academic All-American.* He couldn't have spelled library, much less have known where it was on the campus. So, the creative use of the vulgarity was not considered by my brother or me to be an example of anything more than a poor vocabulary.

This is not judgmental. Neither Steve,

nor I, had virgin ears or mouths. We'd played ball. Been in locker rooms. The truth is that under a pile on a gang-tackle once, when an opposing player tried gouging out my right eye—the f-bomb erupted from my mouth hotter than volcanic lava. The line judge called a 15-yard penalty against me for unsportsmanlike conduct. The gouger got off scot-free. Today, if the f-bomb use led to a penalty, football games would last longer than an Indian cricket match.

Suffice to say, the f-word wasn't used as part of the everyday vocabulary of erudite Americans in that time long ago. It leaked out sometimes in emotional situations, but never into polite conversation. Now the use of it as all eight-parts of speech is no longer a record held by a defensive lineman—it is a record held by many, as they say. Sadly, too many to count.

In the last few years, political movements were all about policing hurtful words, while mainstreaming the F-word. When members of the United States Senate and House of Representatives routinely F-Bomb their way through speeches, it unhappily either says something about the failure of the education system or about the quality of people who call themselves leaders.

My wife and son have come up with some excellent F-words that, when used, will make people better.

Introduction

There's More Than One F-word

Beth Townsend

"Mom, you are going to love him. You've got to go watch his last video."

My son and I love to talk shop, often discussing innovative new strategies or recommending books to each other.

We always like to share tricks of the trade about leadership, persuasion, and communication. We also discuss business trends—who's doing what in the world of sales, and productivity. So, imploring me to watch a video clip of a sales coach he'd started following was routine. So I did.

Wow! This coach had thousands of views and thousands of followers—a highly successful business influencer. But as I listened, for me, his message was lost in a flurry of one word. That made me ask myself, is this where we are in the world now?

His information? Top-notch. His energy? Electric. His physique? Chiseled. His wife? Gorgeous. But his language? Vulgar.

It is one thing to sprinkle in a little bad language as a Tik Tok influencer. But as a business influencer? Have the standards of professionalism changed that much? Or, sorry, sunk that low?

Our country has become so desensitized to profanity that the F-word is now acceptable.

Yes. That F-word!

Not just once, but over and over? In every sentence, repeatedly, trying to emphasize the importance of what they were saying. They are fast-talking auctioneers, F-word going once, F-word going twice, F-word going three times. SOLD to the woman with the F-word.

For two or three days, I continued to

follow the F-word coach. Perhaps the first video was an anomaly. Maybe he was just having one of those days that day. We all let a bad word fly here and there in an emotionalized state. No. Repeated F-words were standard.

A few days passed. Rhett asked me how I liked the coach's content. "Well, son, I unfollowed him. I cannot take that many F-words in that short of a time period. What does anyone accomplish with that kind of language?" Obviously, he wasn't bothered by it.

"Yes, that's true. He does use a lot of colorful language," my son responded.

The mother in me wants my son to follow the kinds of people who will teach him how to be his best and further his career and deepen his character. Not someone teaching him that the F-word is common vernacular.

And when it came to that coach...The parent in me wanted to speak to the parent in him. The mom in me wanted to talk to the mother of their young kids— who was also his business partner and co-influencer. Those young children will grow up and see those videos one day. Are they OK with the content? Is it just the money that matters?

Good things often come from not-so-good things! My initial shock took me to a deeper need for an adequate response. A call to action. It inspired me with an idea for my next book. It was an instant idea, as if it became a must in that moment. This would be my third book, my first business book. As a professional business and sales trainer, I felt I could add to the topic of good old classic communication.

My son and I laughed about it as we discussed it.

"I'm thinking about writing another book."

"What book are you thinking of mom?"

The title had emerged easily. Simple and straight to the point. "There's More Than One F-Word."

Rhett loved it and jumped on board. "I'd like to write it with you."

So, here we are: co-authors.

A blend of Baby-Boomer and a Millennial. Mother and son. Woman and man. Time for an outline.

We sat down with our iPad® in hand, sketching out innovative F-words.

Alternative power words that get people excited. Pumped without profanity. Creative and classy communication.

As a child, I didn't hear many curse words. Mostly those started in middle and high school when kids thought profanity would make them sound grown up and cool. Back then, bad words were bad words. The F-word? The "baddest" of the bad words. Maybe even a getting your mouth washed out with soap bad word. Yes. For you Millennials...that was a thing back in the day.

My opinion, shared by many, was that if people's speech was laced with curse words, they didn't really have much to say. For me, it still rings true. But unfortunately, our culture has reached a place where shock value gets attention. Temporary attention. Some people will say anything to go viral. Need I remind anyone that Covid is a virus? Not saying the F-word won't kill you. But it is a sign of something unhealthy.

I'm a back-to-the-basics kind of girl. I'd like to think of myself as a skilled communicator. Your words matter. Every single one of them.

Choose who you are.

Choose who you are not.

Once it was known as the "F-bomb." Now that it's gone viral, it's just the F-word.

Do you need that word to get someone else's attention? That's a big fat NO!

But Rhett and I are going to send you some other F-words that will make you better at your business.

Better at:

Leadership.

Communication.

Persuasion.

Because there's more than one F-word.

Flammable

Living on Fire

Rhett Townsend

"Are you ready for the fire? We are firemen. WE ARE FIREMEN! The heat doesn't bother us. We live in the heat. We train in the heat. It tells us that we're ready, we're at home, we're where we're supposed to be. Flames don't intimidate us. What do we do? We control the flames. We control them. We move the flames where we want to. And then we extinguish them."

Teddy Atlas, the newly hired trainer for boxer Timothy Bradley, passionately yelled in their corner before the 9th

Round of his Welterweight Title Fight. Everything was on the line, his entire life's work...countless hours...his blood, his sweat, and his tears.

In these decisive, fiery moments, our life stories are written...their resolution, entirely up to us. Who are you in the face of pressure, in our soul's flashes of daunting adversity looming largely in our mind and spirit? Who are you submerged in the fire?

"Rhett, this way, hurry!" My dear friend Riley yelled my way during a cool, misty desert night in the Utah Backcountry. We were in Glen Canyon, an extremely remote plot of public land in Southern Utah, encapsulated by the vast Navajo Reservation.

The crisp summer air bounced off of Lake Powell like shards of glass crackling on polished steel. Surrounding the dreary night was an unknown precursor to the tribulations we soon faced. About an hour before, as a pink and purple aura dyed the sky, another friend Caroline suggested, "Let's climb that mountain. This view is too great not to see it from such a beautiful vantage point."

The restless wind whistled.

The sandy brown dirt ruffled beneath our feet as we walked across a baron strip of land, where about four hundred yards away jagged rock elevated furiously like a broken stairway to Heaven.

We were eighteen years old at the time, having freshly graduated high school. We had a group of friends that no normal person would characterize by being "responsible."

We ascended quickly, but not as fast as the descent of the dark of the dreary night. Not a soul for miles, just the ambiguous howls and sounds of the desolate desert. As we reached the top and looked down, we realized what we had done.

There was about a foot of loose rock and pebble that bordered a limestone wall ten feet high, and below the narrow pathway dropped into a free-fall to death through several hundred yards of unstable stone and monolith down-slope.

"Riley, don't move. I'm coming." I responded.

Miles, Andre, and Peter, three of our other friends accompanying us on the spontaneous mission, were out of sight. They climbed up a different rock face, but we were now separated, only reachable by sound. We could hear they were okay, but couldn't reach them without severe risks.

We were alone, our fate closing in quickly.

As I approached Riley, hugging the constricted space for dear life, looking down into the Jaws of Death, I heard a rumble. About ten feet down on the same pathway, Caroline tumbled. She fell towards her death in the span of a breath.

As I blinked back into reality, I saw her back against a triangular rock about five feet off of the broken passageway. Without such divine placement, she was destined to fall an endless distance through boulder and loose limestone on a highway to hell.

I moved as quickly as possible and picked her up. Together we approached Riley, moved horizontally down the slender path to a place safe for descent, and headed back to camp.

"The Butterfly Effect" is a principle of psychology, which states that in one moment of our lives, or in a greater sense, each and every moment in history, is dictated by small changes that sway the course of our planetary existence. The principle states that if one butterfly flaps its wings in a decimal size difference, all of history is completely altered in a different direction.

These moments exist in every phase of life, just as it did on that fateful night in Glen Canyon. Butterfly moments also appear as large as the underestimated Mamluk army of 12th Century Anatolia, deterring the Mongol Horde led by the infamous Khans from passing through Modern-Day Syria on its way to Europe. This unlikely victory preserved Middle Eastern and European history alike as we know it, and is a glowing example to the fact that if one small difference occurred in their battle, and the result was different, none of human history would be the same.

Butterfly moments are also reflected in the small daily disciplines we keep. These can be as simple as having a daily morning habit, and after doing it for a year, but missing a solitary day, the way that habit is instilled in our mind, starts at zero. That way when the important moment comes, just like it did on that cliffside, your mind is prepared to act, not to panic, but to solve problems, and in certain cases, to save lives.

"The Butterfly Effect" boils down to moments when we are submerged in the fire. The moments we are tested beyond all previous thought of possibility. The moments where everything we ever believed in is shoved in a guillotine and put to an unfair trial.

What decision will you make? Will you crumble in the face of pressure? Will you decide that your army is a tenth of the size, and that the only possible result is sheer death and destruction, leading you to run and hide?

When we evolve into an understanding of who we are in the fire, we become on fire. Becoming on fire means living with vigor, striving for excellence in all things, and having a defining purpose that acts as a compass for our lives as we navigate the vast ocean of our existence.

President Theodore "Teddy" Roosevelt is famous for his brief yet eternally powerful speech, known as "The Man in the Arena"

"It is not the critic who counts; not

the man who points out how the strong man stumbles, or where the doer of deeds could have done them better. The credit belongs to the man who is actually in the arena, whose face is marred by dust and sweat and blood; who strives valiantly; who errs, who comes short again and again, because there is no effort without error and shortcoming; but who does actually strive to do the deeds; who knows great enthusiasms, the great devotions; who spends himself in a worthy cause; who at the best knows in the end the triumph of high achievement, and who at the worst, if he fails, at least fails while daring greatly, so that his place shall never be with those cold and timid souls who neither know victory nor defeat."

The transition from making the decision on who we are in the fire, to becoming the fire, and finally living on fire, is defined by action. Massive amounts of imperfect action define success. However, success is meaningless without moving in the right direction.

Being in the fire isn't about winning every fight, but fighting every fight in the direction our burning souls desire. Our shortcomings and failures in such a fire propel us to heights we never before knew.

Who we decide to be in the fire is up to us. The direction we move in that fire is up to us. It takes learning through weathering the significant storms of life's unpredictability. Becoming the fire is a conscious awareness of who we've become in the fire, through it, and who we become on the other side.

Surrounded by the flames, will you decide never to go back to our old self? Living on fire is our journey's final destination, and it is the only way we can reach the enlightenment of our true potential.

How did Timothy Bradley respond in the fire? With a 9th Round technical knockout to remain the World Welterweight Champion.

In a world where the average stay lukewarm, live on fire. For this is the only way we can truly live.

Festive

Find Your Festive

Beth Townsend

Ask anyone who's been a guest in my home to describe it in one word. The answer is almost always the same: FESTIVE. It's decorated for whatever season is upon us—and in Louisiana, there's always something to celebrate.

Christmas is my favorite, no question. My mom made it so special for us, and it always put her in the most festive mood. Like mother, like daughter. But in our home, festive might also mean undecorating the Christmas tree just enough to convert it into a Mardi Gras tree—because why cut the season short when you can extend it a few more months? If I ever figure out how to turn a Mardi Gras tree into a Fourth of July tree, I will. And honestly, the Christmas tree is already up before Thanksgiving. Maybe next year, I'll put it up in time for my fall décor. Might as well make it year-round.

Once, I led two training events in one day—one in the morning for one client, another in the afternoon for a different company.

The first session was exactly what you'd expect: a nice meeting room, a big whiteboard, the right people in attendance, and the boss taking notes. It went well. I brought the energy.

The second session? A whole different experience. On the elevator ride up, I could feel the bass vibrating through the ceiling. "Oh, I hope that's where I'm going!" Sure enough, when the doors opened, We Will Rock You was blaring. FESTIVE. People were in capes. The whole office was decked out in a superhero theme—balloons, cupcakes, bright colors everywhere. I knew about the promotion they were running, and my training outline was set up to support it. But I hadn't expected this. It was fun. And so very festive.

A previous Gallup poll on the "State of the Global Workplace 2023" revealed some sobering statistics:

59% of workers are "quiet quitting" (not engaged).

18% are "loud quitting" (actively disengaged, however still collecting a paycheck).

Low engagement is costing the global economy nearly $9 trillion annually.

Even more telling? 44% of employees reported feeling stressed at work, and 51% were actively job-hunting. In my corporate days, I interviewed countless candidates who had never told their current boss they were unhappy. That's peak disengagement—on both sides.

If a supervisor is surprised when someone quits, that's not just a red flag. That's a five-alarm fire. It means there's no communication, no shared vision, and no sense of value for that employee's role. And we all know that replacing a good worker costs far more than keeping one. Not to mention the disruption to team momentum.

Now, I'm not saying you have to put on a superhero cape every day. But if you're not doing something to make work feel festive—where people actually want to spend 33% (or more) of their day—then don't be shocked when your best talent walks out the door. We live in an age of high anxiety, where people feel disconnected. Work has to mean something beyond a paycheck.

Let's be real: Monday morning dread is the ultimate company culture test. Between my two training sessions that day, one was good. The other? FESTIVE!

Enthusiasm is contagious.

A well-managed and enthusiastic workplace fosters friendly competition, drives better performance, and creates an environment people don't want to leave.

Yes, work is work. It's not supposed to be all fun and games. But if it's only work—without recognition, without energy, without some "atta-boys" along the way—people start looking for greener pastures. And "greener pastures" usually means somewhere that feels more fulfilling.

In my property management career, my teams leased apartments. In Atlanta. We had a lot of competition. Everyone had a "special." Every complex had amenities. But at the end of the day, we weren't just selling square footage.

We were selling home.

Investors loved marketing plans, detailed budgets, and spreadsheets. Those were fine. But my real focus, as a leader, was always: How do we make this community feel more like home than the place next door?

And let me tell you—there is nothing basic about the basics.

First impressions start before a customer walks in. Have they driven through a well-kept property? Is the landscaping perfect? Is the curb appeal welcoming?

And once they do walk in—what do they find? Happy engaged professionals? Or people just going through the motions? A beautiful property with unmotivated staff won't make the numbers the investors expect.

Then there's the final hurdle—the model home itself. Freshly painted door? Patio swept? Could they move in today? Or...cobwebs, creepy crawlers, and that faint musty smell of neglect? It all matters.

The same applies to today's digital world. Online tours, online reviews—customers are deciding before they ever step foot in your business. If your online presence is confusing, stale, or bland, you're already losing.

And what does festive have to do with selling homes? Everything.

My husband and I have been considering downsizing. We visited a cute gated community. The sales office had a sign: "Back in a few minutes." The door was unlocked, the weather was cold and wet, so we went inside.

When the agent finally returned, he was nice enough. But no effort to connect. No questions. Didn't ask our names. Didn't take our number. It was a forgettable experience.

That conversation could have been ongoing. Instead, I doubt he'd recognize us if we bumped into him at the grocery store. No connection. No relationship. No opportunity to meet our needs.

The model unit itself? Very nice. Probably exactly what we were looking for. But the atmosphere? Dull. No fresh coffee. No cookies. No music. No football game on TV. (Wait—no TV at all?!)

Nothing festive about it.

So what did they do? What most companies do—lower the price. Instead of creating an irresistible environment, they made the product cheaper. Maybe next time they drop the price, we'll go back.

But at my house? My festive is real. And people know it.

That's why, in my career, it made sense to bring that same energy into the workplace. Because at the end of the day, we weren't just selling homes. We were selling the feeling of home.

And of all the "F-words" in business, Festive is the opposite of Fake.

People need fun. But they don't need fake people pretending to be perfect.

Practicing festive—day in and day out—gives you an edge in your career. At its core, festive is about gratitude. And gratitude is an attitude. It draws people in.

So, define your festive.

What makes you, you?

What brings out the best in you?

What environments make you come alive?

What conversations make you stronger?

Are you building relationships at work? At home?

And, bottom line—is work working for you?

Or is it time for a little more festive?

Fluidity

"Be Water, My Friend." Bruce Lee

Rhett Townsend

"Do not deviate from the plan. We have been running this business the same way for fifty years, Rhett. Haven't you heard the old saying, 'If it ain't broke, don't fix it?'" The old man yelled back my way. Mr. Drake was a sixty-year car business veteran, and he was, as they call it, set in his ways.

"Yes, sir, Mr. Drake, I completely understand." The business is changing, and forever will be. We are supposed to change, to evolve, as is the world of business.

Isaac Newton's Third Law of Motion states that "for every action, there is an equal and opposite reaction." Change is inevitable, but hiding from it is deadly. Being fluid means acting purposefully toward the future, pivoting constantly, evolving continually.

"Now let's get back to work, Rhett. Dial for dollars, and bring the damn customers here. We can't sell them when they aren't in the store!" Mr. Drake replied, and all I thought about was Digital Retailing, Artificial Intelligence, the transformation of the customer experience, the evolution of company culture, and how the definition of "market share" changes so rapidly with time.

He was the living example of another saying... "You can't teach an old dog new tricks." And you can't, but that doesn't mean you cannot be an "old dog" and an innovator. One can, but it takes a direct and intense intentionality to strive forward and start at zero daily.

As stated in Newton's law, for us to change, there must be a proponent of such change. Such a change starts with us, and when pursued correctly with vigor and agility and spreads like wildfire to all those we interact with, burning a sense of purpose into the soul of the world.

One of my mentors, Coach Burt, used to tell me, "It all goes to zero at midnight... and eventually winter is going to ask what you did all spring and summer."

What did you do all spring and summer? The same thing you did the year before?

I loved Mr. Drake. While working for him, his stories and ideas always taught me something. But there was only one of us that felt that way about the other. He loved the way I worked, but could never understand the way I thought.

Robert Greene writes, "By taking a shape, by having a visible plan, you open yourself to attack. Instead of taking a form for your enemy to grasp, keep yourself adaptable and on the move. Accept the fact that nothing is certain, and no law is fixed. The best way to protect yourself is to be as fluid and formless as water; never bet on stability or lasting order. Everything changes."

Fluidity is the modern era equivalent of De Soto's infamous Fountain of Youth. We must seek it, be willing to die for it, and stop at nothing to find it. If found, our life will never be the same again. Just as De Soto's Spaniards demonstrated, when we believe in something enough, there is nothing that will stop us from relentlessly pursuing such a valiant mission.

In a world of the unknown, death silently stalks us, creeping closer with every step. Horrible atrocities loom above as loud lavender tones streak across the sky; as the sun creeps over the western horizon, we must constantly revert back to formlessness as our safe haven.

Fluidity is driven by curiosity. Curiosity kills complacency. An individual that lives by the standards of functional fluidity will always be curious, and therefore never complacent. A complacent individual is a dead one.

Albert Einstein is famously quoted, "When you stop learning, you start dying." This statement should be a cornerstone of every human life. However, while book learning is ever important, many dumb this quote down well below the meaning Einstein bestowed upon it. Learning is done in many ways, but in its most productive fashion, is done through experience.

In all things, Seek Discomfort. Being comfortable means growing complacent. It means we lack curiosity and that our minds are shaping into a rigid form that can never be undone.

A mindset of fluidity, to always adapt and overcome, to always find new ways, foster innovation, and turn the world forward in direction, powerfully brings us one step closer to greatness.

"Mr. Drake, I appreciate all the lessons I learned from you, sir. I will take them everywhere I go in my career. Your guidance and lessons have me equipped to handle anything, and I can honestly say, without you, I would not feel the same." It was my final day at the family owned dealership I was raised in. After five years, it was time to move on.

We should all strive towards accomplishing a similar mission, to row the boat together in the same direction. However, in some instances the culture you want to build isn't the one that exists. Yes, we can change culture internally, but to know ourselves is to know our worth, and our worth will always shine brighter in a place where we tear down the wall of comfort and normality, fight the status quo, go beyond what we know, and use a curious heart to become beautifully formless.

Fluidity means in all situations, we will find the creative and most beneficial way to move forward. Fluidity means we will stop at nothing to do the right thing, the right way, each and every time.

My experience in Baton Rouge selling cars was amazing, and I loved our team and what we accomplished. Taking a store that had never earned the stripe of being the number one volume Chevrolet Dealer in Louisiana, and rewriting history was special. But there's a time and a place for everything, and it was time for me to move on.

Only dead fish go with the flow, but to assume formlessness with intentionality rises us to the ceiling of human potential.

"When you want to fight us, we don't let you and you can't find us. But when we want to fight you, we make sure that you can't get away and we hit you squarely... and wipe you out... The enemy advances, we retreat; the enemy camps, we harass; the enemy tires, we attack; the enemy retreats, we pursue." Mao stated on the concept of warfare.

Life and business alike are war, and to understand how to fight is to understand how to live. Being predictable is to walk into a field of lava, rather than being formless and floating beyond it.

If we are well understood and predictable, all the traps of the world will entangle us, strangle us beneath their boots, and cover us like a wet wool blanket. However, when we elevate to formlessness away from worldly understanding, there is nothing we cannot do, and no place we cannot go.

Frost famously wrote, "Two roads diverged in a wood, and I—I took the one less traveled by. And that has made all the difference."

Fight, take the road less traveled, despise the status quote, reject comfortability, deny the stubborn old dog, and transform the world through the innovation of formlessness.

Fear

Face Your Fear

Beth Townsend

Fear is a scary!

Or is it?

Fear is a force. That's certain.

It is a positive and a negative.

Fear has an important job to do. Keeping you alert. Something you're anticipating. Something you're aware of being a danger.

Fear is an emotion.

Deserving respect.

It can be strong, unpleasant. Causes anxiety. Anxiety, out of control, can ruin someone's life.

Fear can be an asset if it is managed, kept in its proper place. Recognized for its purpose.

In my early twenties, I felt dizzy and went to a doctor. Early into the exam, I was hooked up to a machine, stickers attached all about my body. Why did I need an EKG? I was young. Healthy.

Strong. My only need was to know why I was feeling faint.

Fear gripped me.

That was my first panic attack. In the doctor's office. Having an EKG. Heart racing. Struggling to breathe. Freaking out, certain my death was imminent. The official diagnosis? Strong heart and body. Though thankful for the clean bill of health, fear invited itself into my mind and settled in.

If you never had a panic attack, they are debilitating. Thankfully, I've learned a lot over the years since.

Fear is a problem when it is given room to roam.

Here are three ways to face your fear.

Be alert. As a survivor of both a home invasion and bank robbery at gunpoint, my firsthand experience has taught me the necessity of alertness. People can be violent and dangerous. Watch the ten o'clock news. Pay careful attention to your surroundings. It may keep you out of danger. It is a way to manage fear. You will rarely see me staring at my phone. It puts people in a vulnerable position. Not where you want to be—ever. If the Boy Scout motto is "Be Prepared" mine is "Be Aware!"

Know what is going on around you at all times. God gave our eye's panoramic vision for a reason. We were never created to go through life staring at a four-inch screen. The constant use of technology makes most people clueless about what is happening to their right, left, behind them, or just in front of them. That is dangerous.

Elevate facts over fear. Have you ever read the acronym FEAR; False Evidence Appearing Real? More often than not, fear is based on false evidence—a lack of the facts. Potential unknown outcomes wreak havoc in our thoughts. We let fear have its way because we don't deal with what causes fear.

Festering fear takes control. It seems silly now that my fear of my first EKG led me to leap to a conclusion that I was having a heart attack and at death's door. Facts said differently. I was strong and healthy, but had not been living a healthy lifestyle. That day I faced a truth that I needed to take better care of myself.

Someone I know spent her lifetime with FEAR of flying. Her husband traveled the world with friends. She missed every trip. Another friend feared storms, her husband rushing home from work every time a thunderstorm threatened. Paralyzed by panic, he'd sit with her. Still another friend of mine feared bridges, navigating entire trips just to avoid long, high bridges. 98% of what we worry about never happens. Imagine the effort that goes into managing such strong feelings of fear?

Manage fears. Take an inventory. What are you afraid of? Who are you afraid of? One woman told me she was afraid of her husband. "He gets angry so easily." She was crying. Her strategy was "learned" and wrong. She'd simply shut down her emotions to keep the peace. My question was, "Why don't you let him know how you feel?" She was skeptical. "He won't care. This is just how it is." I kept pressing in. "If you want to be healthy, then walk out of the room when he is in that kind of mood." My suggestion was that she let him know how she'd been feeling, and to let him know her response. "When you are angry, I'm going to leave the room, and you can let me know when you are feeling better." It worked.

Managing relationships is sometimes central to facing fear. If you are afraid of another person—boss, spouse, parent, anyone—write and implement a plan for managing those relationships and the related fears. Yes, it is that important. You can't duck and cover! Sweeping it under the rug makes everyone trip on it. Things don't work themselves out. People work things out. You must think enough of yourself to face the person you fear by choosing to take a stand for yourself. You don't need to fight, argue, threaten or yell and scream. You calmly state a new fact, "I'm going to wait until we can have a more productive conversation." That is an effective strategy with a declarative statement.

Experience has taught me this

powerful principle: Better me = Better we. The stronger I am, the stronger my relationships are. You must learn to stand strong for yourself and calmly communicate with others.

Who's the boss? This is huge! You've got to pre-decide how fear is going to affect your life. Recognize it. Name it. Speak to it. Are you going to let it be the boss of you? Or are you going to be the boss of it? This is a great question deserving of an answer.

If necessary, do 'it' afraid! It is scary to start a business, but each year millions do! It is scary to get married and have children, yet all over the world people are starting families. It is scary to go to the doctor to check on that nagging pain, but if you don't, it will continue to taunt you. It is scary to travel and go to new places, but so many people love to travel and see the world. It is scary to quit your job to fulfill a dream, but people do it every day! Most decisions have some level of risk attached, gather facts and make a decision. Fear will either propel you forward or hold you back.

Fear is a friend.

Fear is an enemy.
Respect fear when needed.
Reject it when it's necessary.
Have a plan!

Feracious

Breaking Ground

Rhett Townsend

"To be, or not to be, that is the question."

Is it really that simple? As easy as Shakespeare makes it seem? What does "being" actually entail? In a life where we do one thing, where we become monotonous, in which we live vicariously through a screen, or through others and do not branch out of our comfort zone... is that really life? Is that really why we're here?

The word Feracious comes from the Latin word ferax, which comes from ferre, meaning "to bear."

To live a feracious life is to cultivate abundance. Although one cannot live abundantly without learning, growing, and pushing themselves with an unshakable urgency of bold intent.

Intentionality is the cornerstone to living as a feracious human, and it is the root of our being. Shakespeare's simple quote in Hamlet drives a powerful message home regarding our ability to choose. How will my attitude be today? Who, today, will I positively impact? Who will I be today, the person I dream of, or will I let my dark side take over?

"Being," as Shakespeare put it, is lived in a state of meticulous consistency of constant variation. This consistency is a discipline few fully grow to understand, but it is necessary to become fully absorbed in a feracious life.

Kaizen is the Japanese principle for continuous growth. "Kai" means "change" and "zen" means "for the better" in Japanese, encapsulating the core philosophy of Kaizen—to make incremental but continuous improvements.

Such improvements result in what

economics is taught as "Compounding Interest." As one continues to invest in a business venture, dollar cost averages pan out, the company's growth continues, and what seems like years of static growth accelerates beyond belief overnight.

Practicing Kaizen in our daily lives produces personalized compounding interest.

However, continuous improvement goes far beyond improving at one thing. If we only grow horizontally, we can never reach our full potential. Vertical growth takes us to unknown places physically and mentally, and launches us to uncharted abundance.

During a summer in my college years, I was awarded a scholarship opportunity through a connection of my beautiful mother to travel to Israel to embark on an Archaeological Dig at a largely unknown site called Tel Hadid.

I went with New Orleans Baptist Theological Seminary, a small ecclesiastical school in which most of my fellow attendees were decades older, and dramatically more conservative in their schools of thought. It should go without saying that being around those with differences is an invaluable and necessary part of life's climb to greatness, but unfortunately, in today's society, the status quo is this principal's antithesis.

Unknown to me as I flew across the Atlantic, over Europe and Turkey, and into Tel Aviv, I would be greeted with a pleasant surprise. NOBTS was partnered with Tel Aviv University, fostering archaeologists and brilliant minds from every end of the globe.

The first night at dinner, I was sitting alone eating Baba Ganoush trying to fully understand what the next month would really entail. I was across the world, alone, a young, and sometimes to my detriment at the time, fearless teen. I was approached by a jovial and powerful presence, Alexandria, who would soon be known to me as Alex.

Alex was pushing boundaries never before pushed in the Middle East. She was a powerful figure in the World of Archaeology, a field historically dominated by men, especially in that region of the world. Alex was one of those people that hardly seemed real, almost like an angel.

She told me after an hour-long conversation of personal discovery, "Rhett, in a world full of horses, you're a unicorn." This simple compliment will stay with me forever, but over the next few weeks, I grew to understand this was the only way to even begin to try to describe her.

She chose me to be at her site, AA Upper, as Tel Hadid was divided up into six segments of which we would soon break ground.

Tel Hadid was excavated out of necessity twenty years prior, as the first highway between Jerusalem and Tel Aviv was constructed. During that excavation, there were Assyrian tablets holding loan documents and real estate transactions found, hailing from eight centuries before the Birth of Christ.

Archaeology is an incredibly extensive undertaking. A "Season", the time in which the actual digging takes place, is only four weeks. The rest of the year is spent either researching where exactly within the sites the pick axe will hit the clay, or researching findings from the previous dig. The crew I had the pleasure of growing incredibly close to that summer had spent the last years, and their more tenured team members decades digging at Tel Gezer. Everyone knew there was gold under Tel Hadid's untouched, rustic earth, but for them, it had to wait.

Now, it was our time, my time. How did I even get here? I had no background in archaeology whatsoever. Just an arrogant college kid who thought he knew more about history than he really did.

"Rhett, darling, we're going to uncover history here. History never before seen, never before known, use the axe gently, you never know what you're standing on top of." Alex was a great teacher, one I'll forever admire. She taught me countless life lessons, and endless lessons of the practices of archaeology.

Being Feracious, bearing fruit for others, is not a one-way street. Feracious individuals live life reciprocally. Living a fertile life is living a life with an open mind, an open heart, and a spirit of adventure.

That "season" of my life changed my world. Being with Alex every day from sunup to sundown, and most evenings well past sundown, exposed me to the true beauty of the world. Politically, we had vastly different schools of thought. However, we never once argued. We bounced ideas off of each other, grew with one another, and broke ground together.

Breaking Ground in the world of archaeology is important. My pick axe was the first in the ground at Tel Hadid in two decades, but the ground that broke most importantly for me that hot, Mediterranean Summer, was not in the sacred, hallowed grounds of Hadid. The most important ground broken that year was within myself. Thanks to Alex, who allowed me to grow into a feracious human, open to learning from others, putting my arrogance aside, learning new skills, but chiefly in adopting a new mindset of fertility.

Leonardo Da Vinci is a prime example of living a feracious life, exemplifying the principles of Kaizen and compounding interest through action. Leonardo's diverse accomplishments and contributions spanned multiple disciplines, reflecting his status as a quintessential Renaissance polymath.

Da Vinci's Artistic Mastery will live forever. His oeuvre includes some of the most celebrated paintings in all of art history. The Mona Lisa is renowned for its captivating expression and intricate detail, while The Last Supper showcases his mastery in composition and perspective. His works are distinguished by innovative techniques and a profound understanding of human anatomy.

Through meticulous dissections, Leonardo further produced detailed drawings of the body, significantly advancing the understanding of human physiology. Da Vinci's work spanned well beyond art and anatomy into the fields of Engineering and Inventive Designs. He was fascinated by the concept of human flight. Leonardo designed various flying machines, including ornithopters and devices with helical rotors, which prefigured modern aircraft and helicopters. Further, He conceptualized numerous military devices, such as an armored tank propelled by man-powered cranks, multi-barreled cannons for rapid firing, and portable bridges to enhance battlefield mobility.

Such a man will live forever, which we should all strive to do. Living forever is impossible without living a feracious life of everlasting evolution of our inner-being. Living forever is only possible with a constant intentional, proactive lookout for Kaizen, not only in horizontal growth in the things we feel we know, but in vertical growth into the undiscovered crevasses of our own lives.

Finesse

Finesse Isn't Fake

Beth Townsend

Among my sisters, we have an ongoing joke. When one of us becomes the punchline, we simultaneously break into belly laughs. "Oh, that Mississippi accent just leaked out again." One of us sista's just had a real redneck moment.

Don't misunderstand, we are four proud Mississippi mamas. We are also professional women and wives and mothers who've worked hard to overcome small-town mentalities. As a result, we've each developed individual versions of our sophisticated selves.

Moving away from Mississippi helped me tone down my country accent, but it's no doubt my native tongue. When people asked, "Where are you from?" I'd known my country accent was all they could hear. So, I began to work on a more professional voice that made me sound smarter. Or so I thought.

Finesse means, "refinement and delicacy of performance and execution. Skillful, subtle handling of a situation; tactful, diplomatic maneuvering." It's like a game of bridge. There's a method of leading up to a tenace, in order to prevent an opponent from winning the trick with an intermediate card.

Finesse sounds a lot more like sophistication than country.

Calm. Classy.

In twenty-five years of interviewing well-known people, I've interviewed two famous comedians. Both southerners. During the start of their careers, both Jeff Foxworthy and LeeAnn Morgan were advised to get voice lessons to overcome their southern drawl. Each was told they'd have a better chance to succeed if they sounded less country. Yet they're both very successful, partly because of their authenticity and unique ability to make their southern voices sound so funny. "Y'all"—a little southern never hurts anything. Jeff Foxworthy and LeeAnn Morgan are prime examples of finesse.

It's important to never forget where you came from. Choose to be proud of your story, even the tough stuff. While my Mississippi leaks out in my southern accent, I've learned that there is more to me than how I sound. My accent is part of who I am and I'm thankful to be an authentic Southern Belle. I'll turn off a television show when the actor's southern accent is obviously fake. Really? Finesse cannot be fake.

While education can certainly be an excellent teacher, so can personal experience. I have been trained and certified in a classroom and by life experience to handle difficult situations with ease. More often than not, on-the-job training as a leader prepares us to look beyond the surface of any situation to seek how to best understand others under pressure.

My first full-time job was great

because finesse was defined by my first boss. A family man, who was a man of faith, never once preachy at me or to me, instead accepting me where I was. Coaching me. Mentoring me. He was an accomplished man. President of a bank. He had finesse, demonstrated it without words.

For just over two years, he handled me well. Took me under his wing, managing our relationship; skillfully, subtly handling situations: artfully, diplomatically maneuvering. The very definition of finesse!

Few supervisors understand finesse, nor seem to have any desire to skillfully, tactfully, diplomatically maneuver, as they manage people to try to get the very best out of them at work. As an employee, I worked hard for that bank president, never knowingly letting him down because he was good with me, for me, and to me. It was a reciprocal respect. His commitment to me resulted in my commitment to him. There is a popular phrase: "you don't care how much someone knows until you know how much they care." Oft repeated, it has earned its popularity honestly.

A leader's countenance must illustrate finesse. Every word measured, more listening that talking, confident body language, understanding the level of influence he or she has had on individuals and even on entire teams. He, my first boss, never took his role for granted. And I never once saw him lose his cool or become angry.

Then there are the negative influencers? Those have equal impact, maybe greater. Opposites of finesse! I've had terrible bosses and easily remember how they made me feel. Insecure about my future with the company, like I didn't matter to the team. Some managed by fear, they made make their mark too. While performance is mandatory at any job, how the pressure is applied will determine the outcomes.

Years later, in my career, another boss chose me for a senior position, advancing me above many of my peers. It became frustrating because those peers didn't treat me any differently. I'd become their boss, but you'd have never known it by how they acted. When I mentioned this to my supervisor, he taught me an important life lesson. "A title means nothing if you don't earn the respect of your team." My job was to show them I could be a great leader. Many people get promotions only to get a bad case of boss-itus. "I'm the boss now. Do what I say." Most people don't leave jobs, they leave bad bosses. Bad bosses don't have finesse.

High employee turnover can significantly disrupt work by decreasing productivity, lowering morale, and creating gaps in knowledge and skills. Sometimes, increasing workload for the remaining staff, and overall causing a sense of instability and uncertainty within the workplace. This can potentially have a snowball effect, leading to further departures and impacting a company's effectiveness.

Finesse is a learned skill, interacting with others in a way that gets the outcome you're looking for, despite situations that have grey area and a range of potential outcomes. Finesse is the ability to notice what's unsaid and handle sensitive dynamics.

We all lead someone. Reflecting on the leaders in your life and choosing which type you'll become and want to pass down is an important exercise. We spend a lot of time at work. What will others be saying about you twenty-five years from now? People don't forget bosses. Yet too many bosses have little thought about how their actions impacts other people for a lifetime. That isn't leadership, and it is the opposite of finesse.

There's more than one F-word. Finesse is a good one!

Ferocious

Relentless Determination

Rhett Townsend

"In the depth of winter, I finally learned that within me lay an invincible summer."
- Albert Camus

"Yes, sir. I'll be better." I bit my lip, agitated by his negligence in empathy. Even though he had thirty years on me, I knew he was in the wrong. I took the high road and didn't clap back his way.

"You know, if you leave me, you can't make this type of money anywhere else. You need me."

"I understand, sir." Thoughts raced

through my mind like the Monaco Grand Prix, as I was doing everything in my power not to lash out at him.

My place is to make myself more dangerous, more ferocious. Feeding into another's narrative does the opposite. It makes us bound to their thinking, trapped in their will.

When someone does you wrong or screws you over, the only response should be "Thank you, I owe you."

Use wrongdoings as fuel. Use them to get furious, to become ferocious.

Being ferocious isn't loud. Being a killer is quiet. Acting like a sheep, thinking like a lion.

"All Success is born in the dark." I heard Tim Grover say at a conference in Phoenix, longtime personal trainer of Michael Jordan and Kobe Bryant. "The road to paradise begins in hell," he continued, "and sometimes we think as humans we are measured about how quickly we get up when we fall, but sometimes we need to stay down and realize how the hell we got there."

Society's misconceptions about being "dangerous" are detrimental to collective human evolution. Dangerous people have propelled society forward for all of human history. Napoleon, Joan of Arc, Hannibal Barca, Ulysses Grant - a sacred list that continues onward.

Danger feeds the preservation of society, one that may not exist in the slightest without a ferocious leader with a maniacal sense of human worth. Human worth of purpose, not of existence. We are here for a specific reason, and the odds of such an existence are essentially none. Yet, miraculously, we are here. We are alive, and to waste such a life, is the biggest disrespect we can ever enact upon ourselves.

We are taught by modern society to be easy, to lack intense intention toward our vocation, our life's mission, whatever that may be. We are taught that everyone, winner or loser, deserves a trophy, and that by existing, we are winning. I am here to tell you that perception beyond its origin is unequivocally false.

Being ferocious means knowing who you are, also knowing who you are not, as my mother has always taught me, and by knowing our purpose, using it in a direct way to positively affect those around us.

However, without being dangerous, without being ferocious, caring means nothing. Caring becomes as empty as the world's largest, coldest cave, and creates a void in our soul that can never be filled. A lackadaisical approach to life is the first step to death.

The founder of Dubai, Sheikh Rashid, was asked about the future of his country, and he replied, "My grandfather rode a camel, my father rode a camel, I ride a Mercedes, my son rides a Land Rover, and my grandson is going to ride a Land Rover...but my great-grandson is going to ride a camel again."

"Why is that?" he was asked. His reply was,

"Hard times create strong men, Strong men create easy times. Easy times create weak men. Weak men create difficult times. Many will not understand it, but you have to raise warriors, not parasites."

Being a dangerous human being, one that hates to lose more than you love to win, one that lives to see others climb the ranks and win, too, one that will stop at nothing to achieve their goals and bring their team to the top, that is being ferocious.

Words have instilled themselves in language for thousands of years, and society's impressions of such words transform based on the era. Because of what society teaches us today of what self-worth means, the word ferocious is negative.

"Please come to Kris' office, Rhett. We need to speak with you," Johnson quietly told me outside on a cool Tennessee Tuesday evening, after I ran the store for the weekend in his absence.

Something was up. I had told my two bosses, time and time again, that if they changed my position and cut my pay, I would take that as a demotion and resign. They planned to call my bluff. As a twenty-six year old in management in the car business, it is not easy to land on your feet, but winners, dangerous humans that keep society marching forward, always understand one thing.

In a world filled with wagering, where you cannot watch sports without a sensational pressure to gamble, where you can bet on presidential elections, Russian ping-pong, and essentially every other event on earth, people no longer bet on themselves.

Betting on yourself is the key to winning, it is the key to being ferocious. Without betting on myself, my life is meaningless. "Life is but a Vapor..." the Book of James says, and before we know it, our clock has run out. A maniacal sense of human worth also comes with the same sense of urgency.

"The trouble is we think we have time," Buddha once stated. Eastern and Western philosophy each suggest the fleeting nature of time. Without becoming truly ferocious, we cannot understand time's ephemeral being. To become a killer, a relentless being that does not take no for an answer, that cares and sacrifices for their tribe, a ferocious and dangerous individual that can catapult civilization forward, begins with such a sense of urgency.

Without the understanding of now, we can understand nothing.

I was hired at the dealership through a connection to an amazing human, who was the COO of the large auto group. I followed a General Manager there, a great and inspirational human, to the group's worst performing store. We had an inspiring vision to take the store from the depths of the dirt to the heights of the southeastern automotive scene.

I was seeking pressure, seeking a challenge. I was chasing my destiny.

I moved from my home of twelve years in Baton Rouge to a place I knew no one, to an area of the country I was unfamiliar with. After four months of working side by side with the GM I so greatly cared for, he was suddenly ousted with no explanation. Two weeks later, they brought in Johnson and Kris, who, in a sense of core values, I did not see eye to eye with.

"We want you to take the internet director role, Rhett. It will come at a small pay decrease, but we greatly value what you bring to the table, and do not want to lose you." Kris murmured quietly in the silent office while the three of us sat.

"Gentlemen, it has been a pleasure, and I have learned a lot here. But it is time for me to move on." I shook their hands, and to their surprise, left the store to find somewhere my skill set was appreciated at the level it should be.

Betting on yourself is ugly. Winning

is ugly. Winning does not show remorse. It is hard, challenging, and will beat you down in the ring like primetime Muhammad Ali. But winning shouldn't be easy, and betting on ourselves never will be.

"Thank you, I owe you."

Show those that doubt you, don't tell them. Thank them for the opportunity, and walk out with your chest held high, trusting the best is yet to come.

There are two types of people in the world: victors or victims. Ferocious individuals find victory in every circumstance.

Live based on merit of action, and if you're in the wrong room, it is your responsibility to find the right one.

Be dangerous, be a killer. Walk with the unmistakable aura of the fierce lion within beside the jovial presence of the gentle lamb.

Easy life now, hard life later. Hard life now, easy life later.

Which life will you choose?

Flashy

Never Ever Blend In

Beth Townsend

"Do you like these?" I asked my oldest
sister, holding up a pair of jewel-covered,
blinged-out tennis shoes.

"Well, I sure wouldn't wear them,"
she said. Her face said even more.

I grinned, hugging one of the shoes.
"I love them! They're calling my name."

They weren't cheap, but I bought
them anyway—they were unmistakably
me.

Recently, a friend dropped her mom
and me off at a restaurant while she

found parking. By chance, she ended up at a vintage consignment store. On the walk back, I spotted a rack outside with a 75% off sign—music to my ears. And there it was: a $12 jacket calling my name. A total 60s flower-child vibe. No one else would have bought it, but me? No hesitation.

My friend Viki summed it up perfectly: "Only you could pull that off."

Years ago, I attended a conference led by a best-selling author. She exuded class and sass—bold colors, an even bolder presence. Her brand wasn't just her books and conferences; it was her look. When she entered a room, people noticed.

When we met for the first time, it was in a swanky hotel lobby for breakfast. Both she and I were "dressed up." As people wandered in wearing pajamas and slippers, she turned to me and said, "Can you believe how people show up to breakfast?"

Do You Have a Style? I do! I'm comfortable in my own skin and my own style. Blingy, bold, bright—reflecting my personality.

My husband, a business consultant

for years, often said, "Casual Friday was the death of professional dress." I decided to doublecheck the credibility of my source. And even AI agrees: "Casual Friday has led to a broader shift toward a more relaxed dress code in many offices. However, maintaining a professional appearance—even in casual attire—remains important for a positive workplace image."

Does what you wear affect your performance? Research says yes. Studies show that attire influences self-perception, confidence, and mindset—impacting how we approach tasks and interact with others.

Flashy means confident, and ready for success. Does how you dress affect your performance? According to research, yes—absolutely. The clothes you wear influence your self-perception, confidence, and mindset. They shape how you approach tasks, interact with others, and ultimately, how successful you are. Dressing professionally or appropriately for the occasion can boost your self-esteem and sharpen your focus.

Getting dressed starts with getting

dressed for success. Webster's defines flashy as "ostentatiously attractive or impressive." You might not buy blinged-out shoes like mine, but your style reflects who you are and how you want others to see you. Over time, it even becomes an identity marker on your success journey.

Being impressive means making an impression. Make it a good one. Now, let's be real—I'm not suggesting you need to be dressed for a VIP meeting every time you leave the house. I'm often in workout clothes while running errands before the gym or making a last-minute grocery store dash. But no matter what I'm wearing, how I carry myself matters.

Communication is more than f-words. We're constantly communicating, even when we're silent. Studies show that only 7% of judgment in communication comes from actual words, while 38% is based on tone, and a whopping 55% is from facial expressions and body language. That means 93% of what people take away from you is nonverbal!

Next time you're at an airport, take a moment to people-watch. Posture alone speaks volumes. You can see how people feel about themselves just by how they carry themselves.

It's not just what you say—it's how you say it. And here's a wild thought: in a world where most people stare at their phones, you gain an instant edge just by making eye contact when someone talks to you. Simple, yet powerful. A confident handshake? That speaks volumes, too.

Some of the best conversations—the kind that lead to opportunities—happen in unexpected moments. But if your head is buried in your screen, you might miss them.

First impressions are everything. We all know you never get a second chance at a first impression. But here's something even more important: a bad first impression is nearly impossible to overcome, especially in business.

Back when I trained corporate teams, I'd ask, "Would you rather call a business and reach an automated system or a real person?" Everyone, without hesitation, would choose a real person. Then I'd follow up with: "Would you rather deal with a competent automated system or a rude, clueless employee who doesn't care?" Boom. Perspective shift.

Being present and competent matters. And if you want to be a great communicator, you have to first analyze how you communicate. That means getting real about the message you're putting out into the world.

Social media. The workplace. Even sitting on your couch. Who you are is in motion, shaping who you are becoming.

Change is constant, so choose your change. You have more control than you think.

No one chooses your words but you.

No one decides what you read, watch, or think about yourself. No one determines who you are becoming—except you. Turning a challenge into an opportunity.

I remember my first corporate meeting like it was yesterday. I was young, in a room full of experienced executives—most of them men, most of them better educated than me. My only goal? Don't say anything stupid. So I didn't say anything at all. I just listened.

Before the meeting started, the conversation turned to complaints about the new executive hours—7 AM to 7 PM. Most of them weren't happy. They had families and commitments. But me? I was young and single. I could outwork them.

Then the complaints kept coming. I was shocked. Here I was, grateful to even be at that table, and they were grumbling. We'd all signed the same employee handbook. The expectations were clear. This was an opportunity, but they only saw obstacles. And that's when I made my decision.

I'd be the positive in a world of negative. I'd go straight to the chain of command with solutions instead of complaints. I'd work. And while they kept grumbling, I kept climbing. Eventually, I passed them all.

Attitude is everything. A good attitude goes a long way with any boss. You can teach skills, but you can't teach heart. If someone wants to do well, they will do well.

Which brings me back to flashy. It's more than clothes. It's how you carry yourself. Your attitude. Your energy. It's what makes you, you. Even now, as a (technically) senior citizen, I'm still flashy! And yes, when I get dressed, I always dress for success.

Forward

Into the Jaws of Death

Rhett Townsend

"There is no perfection, only life" – Milan Kundera

To live is to learn, and as we live, we learn the fragility of life. Or so it seems... is life fragile? Or is such fragility merely an illusion?

Roman Statesman and Philosopher Seneca famously wrote, "We suffer more often in imagination than in reality."

Such fragility is merely an illusion, a mirage in the desert after weeks without water and sand in your eyes.

Society teaches us to compare, to stress, to cope...to mask our sense of reality in drinking or drugs. Historically, such society has always evolved by way of the doer. Those that defy the status quo and maneuver our world forward at every challenge. Evolution is churned by those who move forward with a delirious sense of urgency and a keen understanding of the commitment it takes to propel one's family, society, or culture.

Moving forward is about putting our preconceived notions of life aside, and charging into the unknown with a willingness to lose everything in the attempt to achieve enlightenment.

"Avē Imperātor, moritūrī tē salūtant," translated from its original Latin, "Hail Caesar, we who are about to die, salute you."

This infamous quote, hailing from Rome in the First Century, gives a glimpse as to what moving "forward" really means. What does it mean? To go forward, to go all in, to give your entire self to your purpose?

The quote was reiterated on the cold, foggy banks of Rappahannock River by

Colonel Joshua Chamberlain of the 20th Maine as the Battle of Fredericksburg commenced.

His troops were to cross the river and charge up a vast grassy knoll into a stone wall fortified by Robert Lee's Army of Northern Virginia, backed by a line of artillery batteries a mile long. The mission's only result would be death, and the famous colonel knew just that. However, Chamberlain knew his duties, and had no other intention than to carry out the charge.

The brave charge was initiated, through a brutal and bloody conflict, resulted in a Confederate victory. However, Chamberlain and his Maine men exemplified their willingness to sacrifice everything and charge forward into the mouth of hell.

The spoils of war would not forget these valiant men, whom the majority's last breaths were taken on the other side of the Rappahannock. The remaining infantrymen, still led by the brave Chamberlain, got their chance at redemption and would be a quintessential determining factor of the Union's Victory a year later at

Gettysburg, and as a further result the Civil War.

Christian Theology teaches us of Agape Love. Agape Love is a deep, sensitive and sacrificial love. This is the love Jesus Christ carried for his Twelve Disciples and others close to him. Agape Love is characterized by selflessness, interwoven with action taking, and defined by willingness to sacrifice on a profound level. What does it mean to truly sacrifice?

To venture forward into our individual life's abyss, into the unknowns that scare us the most... to go all in, to push all of your chips to the center of the table, to sacrifice your life for the vocation given to you by your destiny...What does all of it mean? What is it all for?

"Rhett, there is a clear and important difference between mistakes of omission and mistakes of commission." My Father told me on the phone, it was late at night and I was outside speaking to him on the phone. Living and working in Nashville for Kris and Johnson taught me many things, but without the sound advice from my beloved father, these lessons would have taken much longer to fully absorb.

"Yes, sir. I just wanted to do better. I wanted to win. I really thought this would be my home for a lot longer." I responded to him. This was near the end of my time at the store I dropped everything and moved states for, and we just lost the top volume dealer award by only three new cars.

"I understand, Rhett, but you need to hold your head high. You worked your tail off for this, and whatever the result of your time here is meant to be. You see, there are only two types of mistakes you can make. Mistakes of commission are the result of incorrect action taken. Sure, you didn't get it, and yes, you rushed into taking this offer without properly vetting everything you should, but you went for it. You could have sat on the sideline and done nothing, still lost, and you'd have never taken the jump necessary to learn this wasn't the long-term employer you thought it would be."

I sighed and reflected. Somehow, my father was always right. He is stoic, with a sage personality and a deep amount of wisdom. This lesson, amongst endless others, are lessons I would've never grasped without him.

There are never losses when making a mistake of commission. Wins or Losses, in this regard, can be summarized as "Wins or Lessons." That year I learned a lot, and without those hard-earned lessons I would not be where I am in my career today.

Mistakes of omission can also be characterized by one not doing what they're supposed to do. If you're on a team, don't let the others around you down. There is a stark difference between being proactive and reactive, similar to the classification of making mistakes. Go get it, fail forward, and when you do, be better because of it.

People are counting on you every day - make them proud.

Henry David Thoreau said: "I have learned this, at least, by my experiment: that if one advances confidently in the direction of his dreams, and endeavors to live the life which he has imagined, he will meet with an unexpected success in common hours."

Chase your dreams, hunt down the life you want, stop at nothing, and lean forward into risking it all. For if we do not look death in the face, we do not know how to live.

"Half a league, half a league,
Half a league onward,
All in the valley of Death
Rode the six hundred.
"Forward, the Light Brigade!
Charge for the guns!" he said.
Into the valley of Death
Rode the six hundred."

The first stanza of Alfred, Lord Tennyson's Poem "The Charge of the Light Brigade," gives a glimpse into a trying and defining moment of the Crimean War. The Nineteenth Century British Cavalry Brigade was given false information. They believed they were charging into the rear of the Russian Artillery Battery, yet they galloped towards them head on. Once the command noticed what happened, they were given a choice. Retreat, or continue onward.

"Forward, the Light Brigade..."

What choice will you make when you look death in the face, when life doesn't go the way you plan? When everything crumbles, will you turn and run? Or will you be valiant, charge ahead, and earn a spot in the Lamb's Book of Life, never to be forgotten?

Fast

Fast Isn't First

Beth Townsend

Slow is smooth and smooth is fast. If he said it once, he said it a hundred times. My MMA Instructor explained, "It's not about how strong you are, it's about how you apply your strength."

Even as someone who has worked out most of my life, it was new information. My personality is high energy and full speed ahead. That is how my workouts had always been. Now to consider 'slow' as a sign of strength?

Fast runs in the family.

There were five children, and I was the youngest. And the smallest. Basic logic was at work from the outset. To get the best food? Eat fast. Want to be heard? Talk fast. Want to ride shotgun? Get to the car fast. If you wanted to be first in my world, you had to be fast. That was my early-in- life lesson: to be first for anything, you didn't have to only be fast; you had to be faster.

Now only four of the siblings are left. But put the four sistas in one room, you'd better hold on to your seats. We aren't busy bodies; we are bodies busy. Walk fast. Talk fast. Think fast. Our mom was like that. Even into her late 80s we'd call her and she would be walking at the gym! Faster than the other old ladies and most of the younger ones.

We love the productive feeling that comes from checking things off on the do list. But checking things off before their due date can cost us in the long run. There's a big difference in making a decision and making the right decision. There's also an important difference between checking something off a list and getting the work done right the first time. If it's worth doing, it is worth doing right. The first time.

Fast isn't always first. Have you ever done something stupid just to get it done?

Years ago, I decided to write a book. I'd been a successful speaker and most speakers write books, right?

The frequent travel had made me realize that airports and rental cars aren't glamorous. My solution? Write a best-selling book that would make money and allow me to stay home more with my young children.

That was in 2001. That painfully slow process proved productive over time. My first book was finally published in 2020. While patience may well be a virtue, it's not one of mine. While I was impatiently waiting and writing that first book, a fast shortcut presented itself and I bought it, literally.

A publishing company had signed several big name author/speakers to write a chapter each in a series of books. Then they offered unpublished authors the opportunity to be included in one of the books.

They reached out to me with the deal of a lifetime by invitation-only. On the book cover with two or three NY Times best-selling authors and motivational speakers. "You'll be a published author in three months!" And the offer was at a special price. The next thing I knew, my check was written to get me into a book.

The special offer wasn't cheap. A waste of time, energy and money. But...I had a published book, ten boxes of them with no plan of what to do with them. Most of the copies are still in my garage, unsold, unread, and a great reminder that fast won't make it easier. If it seems too good to be true, it's too good to be true.

Forrest Gump famously said stupid is as stupid does. What I did was stupid. However, let my life lesson teach you a life lesson.

Fast can lead to failure. Not one person was the least bit impressed by my chapter in someone else's book. Didn't sell one copy to anyone other than immediate family. Though I will say, it's a good chapter and prompted me to revisit and refine my back-to-the-basics business philosophy: "Always find a positive!" My purpose principles are solid and have stood the test of time.

Slow is smooth and prompts one to think about and proactively develop a personal process. Do you have a planned approach to how you make decisions?

According to talkingworks.ca, hurry has become a prevalent bad habit. Hurry: The Pathological Sickness of Today's Generation and How to Slow Down, December 3, 2024.

"In our fast-paced society, the notion of "hurry" has evolved from a simple inconvenience to a widespread pathological sickness. The relentless pressure to keep up with demands, both personal and professional, has left many feeling overwhelmed, anxious, and disconnected. As we navigate through the chaos of modern life, it's crucial to recognize the impacts of this hurried lifestyle and explore ways to cultivate a slower, more intentional existence."

One day as I was out running an errand, a kind man stopped me by asking, "Hello ma'am, what is your hurry today?" I stopped, smiled, and we shared a brief but meaningful conversation. "Gosh, I have no idea, I guess I'm just used to being in a hurry!" We had a good laugh and went on our separate ways.

The importance of that conversation was that now, when it's a top-of-mind reminder when it feels like it's time to slow down. At least to slow down long enough to evaluate what I'm producing with my time and talents.

Fast can be fatal. Fast food may be fast, but it's also dangerous! The measurable consequences are literally killing people. Obesity. Heart disease. Diabetes. Liver Disease, Kidney Disease. High blood pressure. And that's the short list.

According to AI more than 1 in 3 men (34.1%) and more than 1 in 4 women (27.5%) are overweight. More than 2 in 5 adults (42.4%) have obesity (including severe obesity). About 1 in 11 adults (9.2%) have severe obesity. The percentage of men who are overweight (34.1%) is higher than the percentage of women who are overweight (27.5%).

Then there's the highway. When another driver zooms by me in heavy traffic, rushing, beeping the horn, weaving in and out of traffic to get one car length ahead of me, I feel bad for their family. It's a good bet that's how they live life. In the fast lane, rushing past everything and everyone that truly matters. The need to get somewhere fast is less likely to be an emergency than a murky mindset of someone who has convinced themselves the hurry habit will pay off. It won't. I know because I know. There are big boxes of unsold vanity-press books in the storage room as an excellent reminder!

Life in the fast lane was a great song. It's just not realistic. Not in the long run. Media marketing messaging leads us to assume the opposite. Fast is sold daily as a panacea for all things and millions of people are buying it. Health in a pill or patch. Productivity in an app. Home cooked food delivered to your door. Life insurance in a click. A chapter in a book.

Do you need to slow down? Is hurry your habit? Step back, practice your process and see your productivity reflect more purpose and less pressure.

Fortune

Navigating the Pathways to Prosperity

Rhett Townsend

"Audentes Fortuna Iuvat," proclaimed by Roman African playwright Terence in his 161 BC play titled Phormio. The play outlined Pliny the Elder, who quoted the now famous line, as he led a fleet of ships towards Pompeii after Mount Vesuvius' viscous explosion buried the city under a blanket of molten rubble, lava and hellacious fire.

The phrase's original Latin, quoted referencing a pivotal and very close to home emotional period in Roman History, looms largely today - "Fortune Favors the Bold."

It is often heard that "luck is what happens when preparation meets opportunity." This common saying is thrown around with lackadaisical nature, but at its roots, it couldn't be more true.

However, its truth isn't rooted in the saying itself, but in the fact that luck isn't really luck at all.

"Luck" does not exist in the world. There is a reason ninety percent of people that purchase lottery tickets are in the bottom ten percent of wealth in the United States. Our society aggressively pushes us to a direction of wanting everything, but giving nothing in return. But what's the point?

What is your "fortune?" Your "destiny?"

It was a hot, humid summer day in Baton Rouge, Louisiana. We were eighteen years old, and as we sat around the rusty metal table in the backyard, sweat beating down our foreheads, Landon looked over at me.

"Rhett, we should move to Wyoming

for the summer." We were students at LSU, and having just finished finals, our next few months were an open book.

"Hell, buddy. Why not? Any particular reason we go to Wyoming?" I responded. I had experience on the road, living out of a vehicle in the vastly uncharted public lands of the Western United States. I was open to such an adventure.

"My mom knows a guy out there. His name is Trip. He owns a fly-fishing company, and from what it sounds like, we can work with him."

Alright, let's do it. Over the next few days, we called our friends Wigley and Caroline and after a week, we made ready for departure. We packed up a rugged, beat down 4Runner with a roof rack so jam packed with nonsense it could've been from the mind of a cartoonist and a green stick shift Jeep Wrangler with a clutch that was hanging on for dear life. We headed west.

Driving across the Idaho border and over the Bridger Mountain pass on that cool June evening into Jackson, Wyoming snowflakes danced off of our shattered windshield like flint sparkling off of a frozen pond. Time stopped for a moment. It was destiny; we were in the right place, at the right time.

After meeting Trip at a local joint, The Bird, he bought us a beer and a burger, and disappeared with the fleeting wind into the mist of the Rocky Mountain night.

One thing he did give us was an idea of where we would live. "Curtis Canyon, boys. Take the dirt road through the Elk Refuge for four miles, and head straight up the mountain." He told us, and that evening after dinner we did just that.

The next day, we drove back into town, bought a local newspaper, and went to the local Cowboy Coffee shop. We called ads, found jobs, and controlled our own destiny. There comes moments in our lives where we have choices, Butterfly Moments, "To Be or Not to Be" moments. That night leaving the Bird was one of those moments. We had traveled across the country with nothing. No money, no resources, just spirits of adventure and feelings of indestructibility.

We spent the next six weeks camping in Curtis Canyon, which ended up being one of the most special experiences I would have never imagined. We met endless characters that were so outlandish they couldn't even make it in the Canterbury Tales. It was a summer of fortune, but without bravery, without chances, without destiny through fortune, would have been impossible.

Reaching one's destiny requires self-submersion into the fire. These principles necessarily compliment the other. Without risk, without that self wager, destiny will allude us. For going to the grave without the realization of one's destiny means you're dead before taking your last breath.

"Fortune Favors the Bold" is likely even older than its two thousand year old reference, and as long as societies function on Planet Earth, it will continue to reign true. Being a bold individual used to be a requirement for longevity in life, however, today it's become a lost art. Today, we want what is easy, what is fast. We want the promotion without working, we want the big pay day without putting in the small, daily work. We want to win the lottery.

Let me tell you a secret - you already did win the lottery. Being on earth and breathing oxygen means you've done so. The odds of existence are next to impossible. Those odds have already been defied. Making it this far and cheating yourself out of the destiny written for you is the biggest mistake one can ever make. Run to the fire, submerge yourself into the unknown. Catapult yourself at the challenges life brings. Come out on the other side a better man or woman. Learn from your mistakes, stay humble in your triumphs, and fight in all things to reach "the other side."

The great transcendentalist Ralph Waldo Emerson wrote, "Shallow men believe in luck. Strong men believe in cause and effect." Fortune, indeed, boils down to cause and effect. As discussed previously in the book, Newton's First Law, the Law of Inertia. Something must change for us to change. For we must act to evolve. We must move toward our destiny to find it. We must dig to uncover our fortune.

Risk defines the human being. Without risk, there is nothing we can overcome. We find fortune and uncover our destiny by overcoming the hurdles in which our journey presents.Suffering through such risks is necessary to find the fortune written before us. Contrary to eastern teachings, "enlightenment" is not the avoidance of suffering. It is the discovery of our fortune through suffering.

Your fortune is yours. "The other side" awaits, but will not present itself without concentrated effort. No one will give it to you - for finding it is a journey that takes most a lifetime. Our life's work is to find such fortune, to uncover such destiny. Are you prepared for it?

The joy, the wins, and the highest peaks of our lives lie in the journey, in the battle, in the fire of life, in our Fortune.

Fair

Life Isn't Fair

Beth Townsend

"Where will I live?" I'd just graduated high school, and my mom had sold our home.

"I'm so sorry honey, I'm broke." Her third marriage had ended badly, and she was moving to Virginia to start a new life. I was seventeen.

It's not like I didn't know we were in trouble. We'd been in financial trouble as long as I could remember. However, I was finally crossing this major milestone. All my siblings were on their own, and it was my turn to grow up. Not only was I about to graduate from high school, but I'd been accepted into the University of Southern Mississippi. It felt good to have a plan, to be going to college with so many of my friends.

Deep down, I knew I didn't have the money. My dad was married again. I'd lost count of how many times. But because he had offered to pay, there was a sliver of hope. This wife had a lot of money.

Sadly, college didn't last long. After a few weeks, I was notified that not one of the university's bills had been paid. Dear old dad. The ninth wife hadn't come through.

I was clueless about student loans, grants or scholarships—though I'd done nothing to earn one. Surviving to this age and life stage was my one major accomplishment. It was sink or swim for me already. Forced to move out of the dorm, needing a new place to live, and a job.

It wasn't fair.

Having tasted what college life for many friends over the next four years made it profoundly worse. At least in my teenage mind's eye.

Finally, getting a glimpse of what normal looked like, only to have it snatched from under me stung. Being thrown into adulthood that young wasn't fair. But that's what happened. Yes, my life has often felt like I was always playing catch-up. In retrospect, "it made me what I am."

Need is a great motivator. I needed a job.

My optimistic, positive attitude and my willingness to work were all I could offer to an employer. That alone was enough to offset my lack of work experience or life skills to get me hired as a bank teller. It felt like an "adult opportunity," though the pay made making ends meet impossible.

That created another "immediate crisis." Surviving and success were synonyms for me. With no other option, I moved in with dad and his wife. It wasn't fair. Or at least it didn't seem fair.

Life there was awful! And I don't use such a heavy word unless it's warranted. They were both sick people. Physically and mentally, with no hope, they were unwilling to do what it took to get better.

Thankfully, within a few months I earned a promotion to head teller. It might have been that some of my colleagues, considering my age and inexperience, might have thought that was not fair to them. Nobody said it.

My own personal and professional development had nothing to do with fair or unfair. Being a part of and leading that team of wonderful people became a solid foundation for my career. My first chance, a solid start to advance.

The bank was a great place to work. Still, the compensation wasn't enough to stay ahead of my bills. After more than two years at the bank, there was an opening for a property manager position in Virginia. It was the same company my mother and an older sister worked.

This job came with both a salary and an apartment! This opportunity proved to be a launching pad. In two years, there came a promotion to multi-site marketing manager. A year later came the chance to relocate to Atlanta, booming in the late 1980s. It was a well-paying job with a much nicer apartment. It also came with a promise of an opportunity to advance. All that required was to do what was expected. At that age, that really meant exceeding expectations.

That gave me a chance to climb that proverbial "corporate ladder." Performing my way to Vice President of Operations, working directly for the CEO. Then that promotion came along when my stint with the company was shorter than some of the other candidates—and certainly I was younger than all of them. Fair? Probably based on one's perspective. I certainly thought so.

During that season of my life, I had accepted as a fact that there were always two C's both consistently working for and against me: Competition and Comparison.

Competition is part of life; we compete every day. Even as kids we had to work hard for that spot on a team or an award in school. Even more importantly, as adults, we compete for promotions, positions, and power.

Comparison is always the catch! We can get stuck on the perpetual hamster wheels of life. Once we start comparing how we are doing to how others are doing, life becomes increasingly unfair.

Now that's a hamster wheel!

Social media is here to stay. For better or worse. It doesn't just impact children and young adults. According to the Pew Research Center, "69% of adults and 81% of teens in the United States use social media. This puts a lot of people at an increased risk of anxiety, depression, or even physically ill due to their social media use." (mcleanhospital.org)

Fake isn't fair. But fake is here to stay.

Without comparing, how can we compete? In today's culture, this becomes a new, but necessary life skill. Anyone that doesn't develop it will feel stuck in neutral every day for the rest of their life. It's our choice.

Why do mature adults compare profiles with that of other people when we know so much of what we see isn't even real? I'm the first to admit to feeling like a failure after spending too much time comparing my posts with other people's posts. How shallow, and yes, I know better.

So much of life and how we feel about ourselves comes back to the choices we make. If we spend hours on social media, we rightly earn the self-confidence dip or temporary depression. It's proven, statistical and factual. It's called doomscrolling for a reason. You reap what you sow.

Discipline is a necessary part of everything we do, from diet to how to invest time to yes, social media absorption. If you truly want to compete, you cannot and must not compare yourself with others. Learn from others? Yes, read books, not social media profiles.

Life isn't fair. Social media is a constant reminder that some people are better off while others aren't. Trying to keep up with the Joneses was hard enough. Now it's keeping up with our 'friends.' It takes a unique brand of self-control and discipline to have a strong presence on social media while not being discouraged by the presence of others. Do what you must to develop and achieve that skill.

"Life isn't fair" means that people don't always get what they deserve or experience equal outcomes, regardless of their efforts, due to factors like circumstance, luck, and inherent inequalities present in society;

essentially, it acknowledges that life often throws challenges and advantages unevenly across individuals.

The good news? If you can and will accept this truth, life isn't fair and won't ever be. You can move forward with the understanding that you are responsible for your life and every decision. You have the great opportunity to understand the power of your potential.

Life feels unfair because it is. Choose to compete and become a winner. Refuse to compare and set yourself apart from others. You can do this!

Closing

The language we choose to use is vitally important in the evolution of our lives. What we think and say alike manifests itself into our reality and paves the way for our future.

The F-word dominates society, and has intertwined itself in every phase of speech and language in America. Have you considered your F-word?

There is more than one! What words will you walk with daily? Will your language be coated in an insensitive aura of negativity?

Your language is your reality. Our F-words should not send us backwards, but should propel us forward.

Knowing who you're not is necessary to know who you are, but how can we begin understanding either?

Everything starts with a thought, thoughts turn into words, and words generate action.

The day my mother and I decided to write this book, we each had a revelation. Hers was intertwined with the shock of the standard of content within modern media. Mine was in the fact that the F-word being thrown around casually was a big deal.

It is! But what F-word is a big deal for you? Who are you to become? The old mantra will live forever - "If it is to be, it is up to me."

It is up to you! It's all on you! We have free will to decide what roads we walk down, who we lend our time to, what words we say in what moments.

You have a powerful ability to impact every human you interact with on this vast, beautiful planet, but how will you do so? Will you smile and compliment, or will you turn away and ignore? A simple choice as this walking down the busy streets of New York City could decide the fate of another person.

When life gets ugly, when it spits in your face, when everything goes against you, who will you be? What person will you become?

Will you be a victim, or will you claim victory?

The choices are ours, and their implications will echo in eternity forever.

"To Be or Not to be, that is the question."

Who are you?

There's more than one F-word, choose yours colorfully and carefully.

ABOUT THE AUTHOR

Beth Townsend is a purpose coach who helps professionals discover their calling and live with intention, while aligning work with purpose. This career is underpinned by three decades of interviewing successful leaders and entrepreneurs from all walks of life who have given powerful insights into how they identified their purpose that gave them the drive to the top. As the international award-winning host of Life on Purpose TV and an award winning author of multiple books, Beth leads people with clarity, confidence, and conviction.

Her practical approach bridges personal growth and professional impact. As a trainer, she has taught thousands of people skills in both the sales and property management fields. In addition, she is dynamic keynote speaker.

Learn more at: **bethtownsend.com** .

ABOUT THE AUTHOR

Rhett Townsend currently leads a dynamic, diverse team of record-setting automotive sales professionals in a Top Five market. As a university senior he was a six-figure earner while working part-time in sales with a Baton Rouge dealership. Upon graduation from Louisiana State University (B. A., Creative Writing & Arabic)—that financial success established his career path. A sales manager at Louisiana's highest volume Chevrolet dealership at 22-years old, his passion became recruiting people.

Strong interpersonal communication skills now allow him to hire, lead, and motivate people at the highest level. And his deep understanding of customer engagement makes him the perfect teacher and coach for young men and women. In addition to his L.S.U. education, he studied Archeology in Israel and is the recipient of the Dale Carnegie Highest Award of Achievement. .